For Patrick, my deaf other half.

&

For Louisa and CODAs everywhere.
What a beautiful world you inhabit.

A Sense of Love

Written by Haley Gienow-McConnell

with

Illustrations by Michelle Boyd

A Sense of Love

This morning I woke up crying,
But daddy didn't hear me call.
Instead he felt my voice on the monitor,
So off he pattered down the hall.
My daddy is deaf and doesn't hear my voice,
But he still understands all my demands.
My daddy knows exactly what I need,
And he says "I love you" with his hands.

Some kids speak to their parents.
This is how they relate.
But talking is just one way
For a family to communicate.
Daddy and I chat in sign language,
And daddy's signs are very wise.
My daddy does not know me through sound.
My daddy knows me through his eyes.

If I want my daddy's attention,
I do not call his name.
I wave my hand, or I flash the lights,
But the meaning is just the same.
Maybe I need some cuddles,
Or I'm telling him it's time for a meal.
My daddy doesn't need to hear me,
Because my daddy knows how to feel.

6

When I play with daddy,
I do not whoop and shout.
I sign the rules, and I use my face,
So daddy isn't left in doubt.
I love spending time with my daddy.
I never let a minute go to waste.
Who needs to know how kisses sound,
When you know how gooey kisses taste?

Daddy's face is scruffy.
Daddy's eyes, they are bright blue.
Daddy is smart, funny, and silly.
I know him through and through.
Daddy knows everything about me,
All the goodness and the woes.
Hearing isn't important.
Daddy smells my sweetness with his nose!

I love my daddy exactly as he is,
Love him unconditionally.
And I know that as I grow,
Daddy accepts everything about me.
Daddy is deaf, it's true,
But that doesn't keep us apart.
Because daddy doesn't love me with his ears,
My daddy loves me with his heart.

Maybe your daddy is deaf like mine,
But still he's lots of fun.
Or maybe you have two daddies.
Or maybe you have none.
Maybe you have two mommies.
Or maybe just one will do.
Maybe you grew in your mommy's tummy.
Or maybe your parents searched and found you.

Maybe your family has no mom or dad,
But is full of lots of kin.
That's just as much a family,
And it's exactly where you fit in.
Maybe a member of your family
Is a person in a chair with wheels.
It doesn't matter what a family looks like,
Only how a family feels.

Families come in lots of colors,
With lots of beliefs and ways to be.
My daddy, he doesn't hear.
Maybe your relative doesn't see.
There are so many different families.
It's impossible to list each one.
So talk about and celebrate YOUR family
Now that this story is done.

The End

REFLECTION:
WHAT DOES YOUR FAMILY LOOK LIKE?

DRAW YOUR FAMILY HERE

ABOUT THE AUTHOR

Haley Gienow-McConnell is a PhD candidate in History at York University in Toronto, Ontario, Canada. Her areas of specialization are American history, deaf and disability history, and cultural history. She lives with her deaf husband, Patrick, and their CODA daughter, Louisa, in Thorold, Ontario. They are all fluent in American Sign Language. Ms. Gienow-McConnell has numerous academic publications to her credit, but this is her first children's book.

Made in the USA
San Bernardino, CA
18 April 2018